INSIDE COLLEGE FOOTBALL™

FOOTBALL IN THE
SEC
(SOUTHEASTERN CONFERENCE)

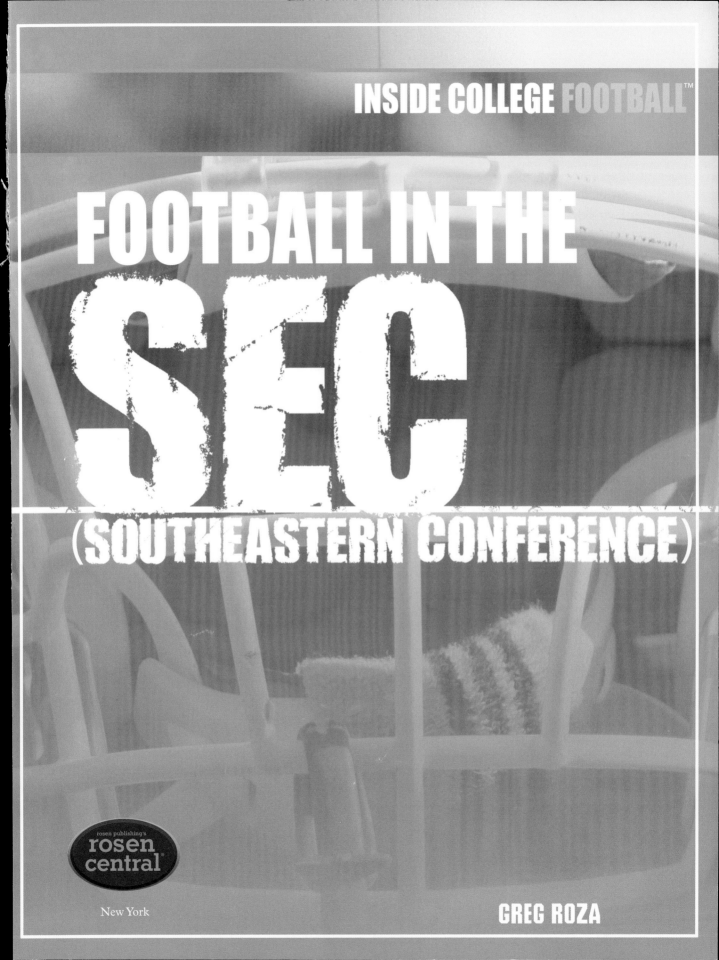

rosen publishing's
rosen
central®

New York

GREG ROZA

For Nick

Published in 2008 by The Rosen Publishing Group, Inc.
29 East 21st Street, New York, NY 10010

Library of Congress Cataloging-in-Publication Data

Roza, Greg.
Football in the SEC (Southeastern Conference) / Greg Roza. — 1st ed.
    p. cm. — (Inside college football)
Includes bibliographical references and index.
ISBN-13: 978-1-4042-1919-9 (library binding)
ISBN-10: 1-4042-1919-6 (library binding)
1. Southeastern Conference. 2. Football—Southern states. I. Title.
GV958.5.S59R68 2008
796.332'630975—dc22

                                                                2007005416

Manufactured in the United States of America

On the cover: (*Top*) On October 7, 2006, players on the LSU Tigers run onto the field before a game against the Florida Gators. (*Bottom*) In a September 2006 win against the Kentucky Wildcats, Florida Gator quarterback Tim Tebow escapes a tackle.

CONTENTS

INTRODUCTION

The Southeastern Conference (SEC) began battling it out on the gridiron in 1933. However, the roots of college football can be traced back to the 1820s. The European games of rugby and soccer were played at Ivy League colleges such as Princeton, Harvard, and Yale. In the 1870s, these schools met in an attempt to create a common set of rules for the game they had begun to call football. In the 1880s, Yale football coach Walter Camp introduced a number of changes to the game. He reduced the number of players to eleven, introduced "downs" to the game, and conceived of the quarterback and fullback positions. It was after these changes that football began to gain popularity with the general public.

Some of the greatest rivalries in college football were born during this early era. Many of these rivalries have endured for over

100 years, keeping fans interested season after season. SEC football in particular has a long tradition of exciting and fierce competition.

Fans of other conferences may disagree, but the SEC is often credited as being *the* premier college football conference. There are some convincing facts to back up this claim. The SEC currently has four coaches who already have won a National Championship. Since the Bowl Championship Series (BCS) began in 1998, the SEC has won three championships, more than any other conference. Nine SEC teams appeared in bowl games at the end of the 2006 season; six of these teams beat their opponents. Many SEC players go on to successful careers in the National Football League (NFL). In fact, at the start of the 2006 pro-football season, there were 266 former SEC players in the NFL, more than from any other conference.

The History of the SEC

In 1894, Dr. William Dudley—a chemistry professor at Vanderbilt College—initiated a movement to organize a Southeastern football conference. Representatives from seven Southeastern schools met in Atlanta, Georgia, on December 22, 1894, to discuss the future of collegiate sports. The result was the Southern Intercollegiate Athletic Association (SIAA). It was the first major collegiate sports conference, and the first college football conference in the nation.

The SIAA

When the SIAA was founded, the seven participating colleges were the University of Alabama, Alabama Polytechnic Institute (which became Auburn University in 1960), University of Georgia, Georgia

School of Technology (known as Georgia Tech), University of North Carolina, University of the South (known as Sewanee), and Vanderbilt. Nineteen other teams joined the SIAA in the next year. Many of the rules established in these early years still exist in some form in the SEC today. Some of the most heated rivalries in the SEC also originated during the first ten years of the SIAA.

As more teams joined the SIAA, the conference eventually stretched from Maryland to Texas. By 1920, the conference had

What Is the NCAA?

In its early years, college football was a violent, brutal game. The rules allowed dangerous plays, and the players lacked appropriate protective gear. In 1905, eighteen players died from injuries they received on the field. Another 159 players suffered serious injuries. After the 1905 season, President Theodore Roosevelt, a passionate football fan, urged athletic directors from across the country to establish a governing body to reform the game.

In response, in 1906, the Intercollegiate Athletic Association of the United States (IAAUS) was founded. The IAAUS held discussion groups and formed committees to change the state of collegiate sports, especially football. Many violent practices were outlawed, such as gang tackling and punching the ball carrier in the face. Other changes increased scoring and excitement, including the introduction of the forward pass. Prompted by the IAAUS, football transformed from a violent and dangerous game into the sport with which we are familiar today.

In 1910, the association changed its name to the National Collegiate Athletic Association (NCAA). Today, the NCAA continues to regulate U.S. men's and women's college sports. It is a legislative body made up of committees and representatives from colleges all over the country. The NCAA punishes schools, teams, and individuals who break NCAA rules. It also awards eighty-eight national championships every year, in addition to numerous individual awards for outstanding athletic achievement.

grown to thirty teams. Throughout the early 1900s, there were disputes between smaller schools and larger schools over whether to allow freshmen to play football. Eventually this dispute led to the formation of two separate leagues. At a meeting in Gainesville, Florida, on December 12 and 13 of 1920, fourteen of the larger SIAA schools split off to form the Southern Conference. The schools that remained in the SIAA eventually broke up to form other conferences.

The Southern Conference

The Southern Conference (SC) was initially comprised of fourteen teams: Alabama, Auburn, Clemson, Georgia, Georgia Tech, Kentucky, Maryland, Mississippi State, North Carolina, North Carolina State, Tennessee, Virginia, Virginia Tech, and Washington and Lee. However, as the fan base for college football grew, so did the popularity of the SC. In 1922, seven more teams joined the conference: Florida, Louisiana State University (LSU), Mississippi, South Carolina, Tulane, Vanderbilt, and Virginia Military. Sewanee became a member in 1923. Duke joined in 1928. With twenty-three teams in the conference, it started to face problems similar to what the SIAA had faced, including disputes over academic standards, recruiting issues, and travel difficulties.

Once again, the conference decided that it had become too large. At a December 1932 meeting in Knoxville, Tennessee, representatives from the SC decided to split the conference into two. The ten teams along the Atlantic Coast remained in the Southern Conference. The other thirteen teams formed the Southeastern Conference, or SEC.

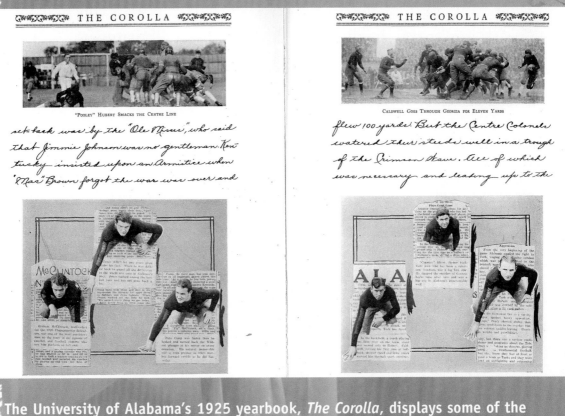

The University of Alabama's 1925 yearbook, *The Corolla*, displays some of the team members and action from the 1924 football season. The top-right photo caption *(above)* reads, "Caldwell goes through Georgia for eleven yards."

The Makeup of the SEC

The thirteen original teams in the SEC were Alabama, Auburn, Florida, Georgia, Georgia Tech, Kentucky, LSU, Mississippi, Mississippi State, Sewanee, Tennessee, Tulane, and Vanderbilt. In 1940, Sewanee—deciding to concentrate more on academics and less on athletics—left the SEC and became a division III team. In 1964, Georgia Tech joined the Atlantic Division Conference, and Tulane joined Conference USA in 1966. This left ten SEC teams. In 1992, Arkansas and South Carolina joined the SEC, bringing the total to its current makeup of twelve. This was also the first year that the SEC was divided into East and West Divisions.

Television and Bowl Games

In the early 1930s, the country was in the grips of the Great Depression and football's popularity had decreased slightly. However, several changes helped the SEC to regain its previous success. The SEC began allowing student athletes to be eligible for financial aid. This helped impoverished young athletes to afford college tuition during the Depression.

Additional bowl games also were created during this time. Since 1916, the Rose Bowl, the "Granddaddy of all Bowl Games," has been played each year between two of the best teams in the country. In 1926, Alabama had been the first SEC team to play in the Rose Bowl (beating the University of Washington 20–19). In 1935, the Sugar Bowl, Sun Bowl, and Orange Bowl were established. The Cotton Bowl was established in 1937. Between 1930 and 1940, SEC teams appeared in fifteen of these bowl games.

During this time period, television entered households and football games were regularly broadcast. Frequent appearances in televised bowl games helped to make the SEC teams more popular. Televised games also allowed colleges to build revenue by making deals directly with national and local broadcasters.

Continued Success After World War II

World War II (1939–1945) reduced the popularity of college football and college sports in general. Many students and coaches volunteered for the military. During the war, a number of colleges

The University of Alabama was expected to lose the 1926 Rose Bowl. Instead, the team beat the University of Washington, 20–19. Fans treated the players like heroes when they returned to Alabama. In this photo, Alabama running back Johnnie Mack outruns two Washington defenders for a big gain.

tried to continue to play football with smaller teams, relying mainly on freshmen and transfer students. In 1943, however, seven SEC schools cancelled the year's schedules due to a lack of players.

Members of the NCAA and the different conferences spent the time during the war revamping rules and regulations. After the war, college football thrived again. Despite differences with the NCAA, the SEC became self-sufficient in 1949. Like other conferences across the nation, it made a great deal of money from ticket sales and contracts with TV broadcasters.

CURRENT SEC TEAMS AND THEIR ACCOMPLISHMENTS

	SCHOOL	TEAM NAME	YEAR JOINED SEC	CONFERENCE CHAMPIONSHIPS	# OF BOWL APPEARANCES	BOWL W-L RECORD
EASTERN CONFERENCE	University of Florida	Gators	1932	6	34	16–18
	University of Georgia	Bulldogs	1932	12	42	23–16–3
	University of Kentucky	Wildcats	1932	2	11	6–5
	University of S. Carolina	Fighting Gamecocks	1992	0	13	4–9
	University of Tennessee	Volunteers	1932	13	46	24–22
	Vanderbilt University	Commodores	1932	0	3	1–1–1
WESTERN CONFERENCE	University of Alabama	Crimson Tide	1932	21	53	30–20–3
	University of Arkansas	Razorbacks (Hogs)	1992	0	35	11–21–3
	Auburn University	Tigers	1932	6	33	18–13–2
	Louisiana State University (LSU)	Tigers	1932	9	38	19–18–1
	University of Mississippi	Ole Miss Rebels	1932	6	31	19–12
	Mississippi State University	Bulldogs	1932	1	12	6–6

The SEC Today

The SEC remains one of the hottest conferences in college football. SEC games are shown on television almost every weekend of the college football season, and SEC teams make bowl game appearances every year. In 2006, the SEC distributed a total of $116.1 million in television revenue to the conference's teams.

On December 2, 2006, the Florida Gators became the 2006 SEC champions, beating the Arkansas Razorbacks 38–28 in the SEC Championship Game. They finished the season with a record of 12–1, and were ranked the second-best team in the nation. They

MOST RECENT BOWL APPEARANCE	# OF PLAYERS TO WIN HEISMAN	1ST ROUND NFL DRAFT PICKS	# OF PLAYERS IN NFL HALL OF FAME	# OF PLAYERS/ COACHES IN NCAA HALL OF FAME
2007 BCS National Championship Game: Florida 41, OSU 14	2	36	1	13
2006 Chick-fil-A Bowl: Georgia 31, Virginia Tech 24	2	25	2	28
2006 Music City Bowl: Kentucky 28, Clemson 20	0	13	1	5
2006 Liberty Bowl: S. Carolina 44, University of Houston 36	1	9	0	1
2007 Outback Bowl: Penn State 20, Tennessee 10	0	37	2	23
1982 Hall of Fame Game: Air Force 36, Vanderbilt 28	0	8	0	9
2006 Cotton Bowl: Alabama 13, Texas Tech 10	0	25	1	11
2007 Capital One Bowl: Wisconsin 17, Arkansas 14	1	26	3	10
2007 Cotton Bowl: Auburn 17, Nebraska 14	2	9	0	5
2007 Sugar Bowl: LSU 41, Notre Dame 14	0	36	6	20
2004 Cotton Bowl: Ole Miss. 31, Oklahoma State 28	0	18	2	11
2000 Independence Bowl: Miss. State 43, Texas A&M 41	0	15	2	8

earned a spot in the BCS (Bowl Championship Series) National Championship Game against the top-ranked Ohio State Buckeyes. Played on January 8, 2007, the Gators, considered underdogs, dominated the Buckeyes 41–14. Gator quarterback Chris Leak earned the most valuable player (MVP) award, and the stunning Gator defense helped the team become the top-ranked team in college football. The win coincided with the ten-year anniversary of their first national championship in 1996, as well as the 100th year of Florida Gators football.

Key Coaches in the SEC

John Heisman, one of the earliest SEC coaches, is honored each year when the NCAA presents the award for the best player in all of college football. Heisman coached at Auburn from 1895 to 1899, leading them to a record of 12–4–2. Every year since 1935, the Heisman Trophy has been awarded to college football's most prestigious player. Heisman, however, is just one of the many coaches who have achieved greatness in the SEC.

Robert R. Neyland

Robert R. Neyland was one of the most successful college coaches. Neyland coached the Tennessee Volunteers from 1926 to 1934, 1936–1940, and 1946–1952. In between these stints, he was a general in the U.S. army, leading troops first in Panama, then in China.

Neyland is credited with turning a lackluster Tennessee team into a true competitor. After a single loss during the 1926 season, the team did not lose for another thirty-three games, until October 8, 1930! Neyland's Vols followed this loss with another winning streak of twenty-eight games. The Vols also won the Southern Conference Championship in 1927 and 1932.

By 1940, Neyland had become the first coach in history to take a team to three successive, major postseason bowl games. During this time, Tennessee won all three SEC

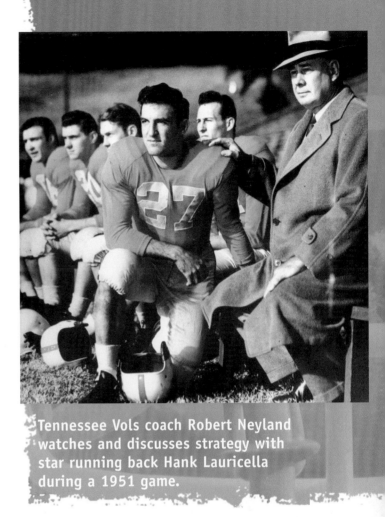

Tennessee Vols coach Robert Neyland watches and discusses strategy with star running back Hank Lauricella during a 1951 game.

Championships and two National Championships. In addition, the Vols kept their opponents from scoring for seventy-one consecutive quarters—an NCAA record to this day. Between 1946 and the end of the 1952 season, Neyland led Tennessee to two more SEC Championships, four bowl appearances, and two National Championships.

Neyland retired from coaching after his last bowl appearance on January 1, 1953. He was inducted into the College Football Hall of Fame in 1956 and is currently the sixth-most successful coach in the history of college football.

Paul "Bear" Bryant

Paul "Bear" Bryant and the Crimson Tide enter Bryant-Denny Stadium circa 1980. Bryant's name was added to the stadium in 1975.

Paul "Bear" Bryant is considered one of the greatest college football coaches of all time, as well as one of the toughest men ever to play the game. (He received the nickname "Bear" after wrestling one at a circus in his hometown.) Bryant played right offensive end for the University of Alabama from 1933 to 1936, and at one point helped the team win 23 out of 28 games. In 1935, he even played a game with a broken bone in his leg.

Despite multiple offers to play professional football, Bryant chose to look for a coaching job. After a short stay with Union College in Jackson, Tennessee, Bryant accepted an assistant coaching position with Alabama. Over the next four seasons, Bryant helped the team achieve a 25–5–3 record.

After serving in the navy during World War II, Bryant returned to coaching. From 1945 to 1957, he coached three teams outside the SEC. He then returned to Alabama as head coach in 1958. Over the next twenty-five years, he coached the Crimson Tide to 232 wins, twenty-nine bowl appearances, fifteen SEC Championships, and six National Championships. His lifetime record as a coach is

323–85–17. During the 1960s and 1970s, no team won more games than Alabama—thanks to Bryant.

Bryant was nominated National Coach of the Year three times, and SEC Coach of the Year ten times. He retired in December 1982 after winning his final game in the Liberty Bowl. He died of a heart attack twenty-eight days later at the age of sixty-nine. Bryant was inducted into the College Football Hall of Fame in 1986.

Steve Spurrier

Nearly three decades before Steve Spurrier coached the Florida Gators, he was their quarterback, in 1965 and 1966. He broke every Florida record for passing and total offense, and every passing record in the league. Spurrier was twice All-American, and the Heisman Trophy winner in 1966. In 1986, Spurrier was inducted

Words of Wisdom

Robert Neyland and Paul "Bear" Bryant were well known as great motivators. Both coaches are remembered for their keys to success.

Some of Neyland's "Maxims":
1. Play for and make the breaks and when one comes your way, SCORE.
2. If at first the game—or the breaks—go against you, don't let up . . . put on more steam.
3. Protect our kickers, our quarterback, our lead, and our ball game.
4. Press the kicking game. Here is where the breaks are made.
5. Carry the fight to our opponent and keep it there for sixty minutes.

Bryant's Three Rules of Coaching:
1. Surround yourself with people who can't live without football.
2. Recognize winners. They come in all forms.
3. Have a plan for everything.

Steve Spurrier discusses a play with quarterback Shane Matthews. Matthews and Spurrier led the Gators to their first SEC championship win in 1991.

into the College Football Hall of Fame for his accomplishments as a player.

Spurrier returned to the Gators in 1990 as head coach. He is the most successful coach in Florida history, helping the Gators to tie, set, and break dozens of records. Also, Spurrier introduced a highly effective offensive strategy that forced other SEC teams to change the way they played.

In his twelve seasons with Florida, Spurrier led the Gators to six SEC Championships (1991, 1993–1996, 2000), and the National Championship in 1996. They appeared in a bowl game eleven years in a row. Spurrier's 122–27–1 record with the Gators was groundbreaking. He is the only major college coach to win 120 games in his first twelve seasons with a school.

Currently, Spurrier is the head coach of the South Carolina Gamecocks. He won his eighth Associated Press Coach of the Year award in 2006.

Sylvester Croom

Before he was a coach, Sylester Croom played center for Paul "Bear" Bryant at Alabama from 1971 to 1974. During this time, the

Sylvester Croom talks to Mississippi State wide receiver Brandon Wright during a game against Louisiana State University in 2004. Although the Bulldogs have struggled since Croom has taken over, he is dedicated to turning them into a winning team.

Crimson Tide won three SEC Championships (1972–1974) and a National Championship (1973). In 1974, he earned All-American honors, and won the Jacobs Blocking Trophy as the best offensive lineman in the league. Today, an Alabama State award is named after him—the Sylvester Croom Commitment to Excellence Award.

Croom returned to Alabama as an assistant coach under Bryant. Between 1976 and 1986, Alabama went to ten bowl games and the National Championships in 1978 and 1979. He also coached many players who would go on to excel in the NFL.

Croom was an assistant coach for five professional teams from 1987 to 2003. Then on December 1, 2003, he was named head coach of the Mississippi State Bulldogs. He made history on this date by becoming the first African American head coach in the SEC. Croom is proud of the accomplishment, but he has stated that he is more dedicated to being the best coach he can be. "I am the first African American coach in the SEC," he said in his press conference after being hired. "But there ain't but one color that matters here, and that color is maroon [the color of the Bulldogs' uniforms]."

Key Players in the SEC

Since the earliest days of football, the South has produced dedicated and talented players. Many SEC players have gone onto successful professional careers—in football and other areas of life.

The Mannings

Some of the most notable players in SEC history are members of the same family: the Mannings. Father Archie and sons Peyton and Eli were all SEC quarterbacks.

Archie Manning played for the University of Mississippi from 1967 to 1969. Archie's best game was in 1969, during the first-ever prime-time broadcast of college football. He threw for 436 yards, ran for 104 yards, and threw three touchdowns in a heartbreaking 33-32 loss to the Alabama Crimson Tide. He played the 1971 Gator Bowl with a broken arm, passing for 180 yards! During three seasons

(From left to right) Eli, Archie, and Peyton Manning share a laugh on the set of a 2006 Reebok commercial. Altogether, the Mannings passed for a total of 26,073 yards during their college careers.

with Ole Miss, Archie threw for 4,753 yards, ran for 823, and scored fifty-six touchdowns. He was inducted into the College Football Hall of Fame in 1989.

Peyton Manning attended Tennessee from 1994 to 1997. To this day, he is the Volunteers' greatest offensive player. While at Tennessee, Peyton passed for 11,020 yards, scored 101 touchdowns, and led the Vols to victory in the 1997 SEC Championship Game against Auburn. He set two NCAA records, eight SEC records, and thirty-three University of Tennessee records. Peyton has continued to be an electric player in the NFL for the Indianapolis Colts. During the 2004–2005 season, he set the NFL record for touchdown passes in one season, with forty-nine. In 2007, Peyton and the Colts won Super Bowl XLI, and he was elected MVP of the game.

Eli Manning attended his father's alma mater, Ole Miss, from 1999 to 2003. Just like his brother and father, Eli had a stunning college career, breaking and setting many school records—including some set by his father. Eli is Ole Miss's current all-time passing leader, with 10,119 passing yards, and he holds forty-five school records. He was named the 2003 SEC offensive player of the year. Today he plays professional football for the New York Giants.

In 2004, the Sugar Bowl Committee began honoring the best college football quarterback in the United States with the Manning Award. (It is named in honor of all three great Manning quarterbacks.) It is the only quarterback award that takes into account candidates' bowl performances. In 2007, the award went to LSU quarterback JaMarcus Russell.

Herschel Walker

Herschel Walker is widely believed to be one of the best football players of all time. Some consider him to be *the* best player in college football history. He played as a running back for Georgia from 1980 to 1982. His first year was one of the best ever for a college freshman. By the end of his college career, Walker had impressed countless people. He set numerous records, including eleven NCAA records, sixteen SEC records, and forty-one University of Georgia records. On top of all his personal achievements, Walker helped the Bulldogs remain undefeated in 1980. The season ended with a Sugar Bowl victory against the University of Notre Dame to win the National Championship.

Herschel Walker sprints down the field with the ball, a familiar sight during his days with the Georgia Bulldogs. Walker became a crowd favorite in 1980 during his freshman year. That year, he scored fifteen touchdowns and gained a total of 1,616 yards.

Walker was an All-American three years in a row, and won the Heisman Trophy in 1982. Many fans thought he should have won it in his freshman year as well. Walker is sixth on the list of all-time leading rushers in college football (in spite of only playing for three years—he skipped his senior year in favor of beginning his professional career). He went on to set many records in the NFL. Walker was inducted into the College Football Hall of Fame in 1999 and will undoubtedly be inducted into the Pro Football Hall of Fame.

Cornelius Bennett

One of the greatest defensive players in the SEC made a name for himself at the University of Alabama. Cornelius Bennett was a Crimson Tide linebacker from 1983 to 1986. Terrorizing quarterbacks, he recorded 287 tackles, 21.5 sacks, and three fumble recoveries.

Bo Jackson: Auburn's All-Around All-Star

Few college athletes have achieved Bo Jackson's greatness. Although the New York Yankees drafted Jackson in 1982, he chose to attend Auburn University. From 1982 to 1985, Jackson wowed college football fans in addition to starring on the school's baseball and track teams. To this day, only Herschel Walker has better numbers for SEC running backs. In 1983, Jackson was named MVP of the Sugar Bowl (Auburn beat Michigan, 9–3). In 1984, he was named MVP of the Liberty Bowl (Auburn beat Arkansas, 21–15). He was awarded the Heisman Trophy after his senior year.

Jackson went on to become an all-star in two professional sports—at the same time! He played football for the Los Angeles Rams (1987–1990), and baseball for three different teams. Although he once stated that he played football as a "hobby," no one can deny that he was one of the greatest athletes ever to play in the SEC.

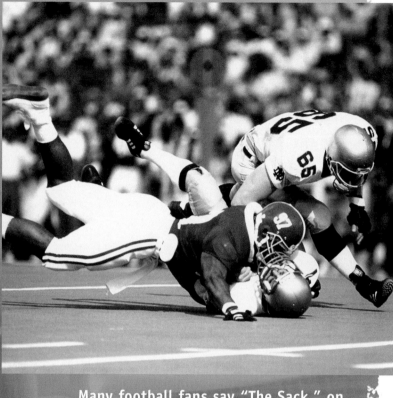

Many football fans say "The Sack," on October 4, 1986 (*above*), is the most spectacular sack in the history of college football. The Crimson Tide won 28–10.

In his most memorable college performance, Bennett sacked Notre Dame quarterback Steve Beuerlein during a 1986 game as Alabama was on its way to its first-ever win over Notre Dame. Alabama fans fondly remember this game-making play as "The Sack." Of course, Beuerlein also remembers it. "It knocked me woozy," Beuerlein says in *Where Football Is King,* by Christopher J. Walsh. "I have never been hit like that before and hopefully I'll never be hit like that again."

Bennett won Outstanding Player awards in the 1985 Aloha Bowl and the 1986 Sun Bowl, both of which Alabama won. In 1986, he was named SEC Player of the Year. Also in 1986, Bennett became the first SEC player to receive the Lombardi Award. For the first time, the honor—originally given to linemen—was awarded to a linebacker. He was chosen seventh in the running for the Heisman Trophy that year, which is quite a feat for a defenseman. In addition, he was named Alabama's Player of the Decade, was a three-time All-American, and was on the 1980s' SEC Team of the Decade. Bennett went on to professional football, playing in four consecutive

SEC Award Winners

The following is a list of SEC athletes who have won national awards. While there are many other awards given away each year, the ones mentioned here are a few of the most prestigious. Many of these players have gone on to successful or Hall of Fame careers in professional football.

Heisman Award: Nation's Best Player

Year	Player	School
1942	Frank Sinkwich (HB)	Georgia
1959	Billy Cannon (HB)	LSU
1966	Steve Spurrier (QB)	Florida
1971	Pat Sullivan (QB)	Auburn
1982	Herschel Walker (RB)	Georgia
1985	Bo Jackson (RB)	Auburn
1996	Danny Wuerffel (QB)	Florida

Butkus Award: Nation's Top Linebacker

Year	Player	School
1988	Derrick Thomas	Alabama
2006	Patrick Willis	Mississippi

Bronko Nagurski Award: Nation's Best Defensive Player

Year	Player	School
1998	Champ Bailey (CB)	Georgia

Lombardi Award: Nation's Best Lineman (Offensive or Defensive)

Year	Player	School
1986	Cornelius Bennett (LB)	Alabama
1988	Tracy Rocker (DT)	Auburn
2004	David Pollack (DE)	Georgia

Super Bowls with the Buffalo Bills (1990–1993). He also played for the Atlanta Falcons and the Indianapolis Colts before retiring in 2000. In 2005, Bennett was inducted into the College Football Hall of Fame. Many football experts expect him to be voted into the Pro Football Hall of Fame in the near future.

4 CHAPTER

Mascots and Nicknames of the SEC

The SEC is well known for fierce competition and dramatic rivalries. The conference also has many colorful traditions. Mascots, for instance, play an important role. These long-standing team representatives have rich and often entertaining histories.

Meet Albert and Alberta

In 1907, Austin Miller, a native of Gainesville, Florida, attended college in Charlottesville, Virginia. Upon visiting his son, Austin's father, Philip, noticed many pennants decorated with the mascots of local schools. He wanted to sell similar merchandise in his Gainesville store. However, the University of Florida did not have a mascot. Austin immediately came up with the idea of an alligator.

In 1957, the first of several live alligator mascots was brought to the university. In 1970, the Gators introduced Albert E. Alligator—a

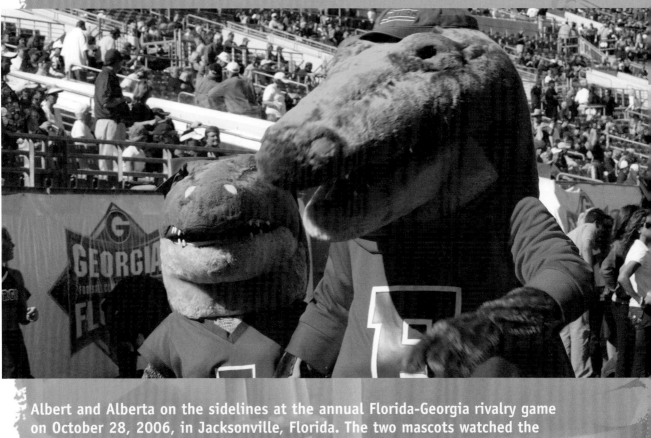

Albert and Alberta on the sidelines at the annual Florida-Georgia rivalry game on October 28, 2006, in Jacksonville, Florida. The two mascots watched the Gators win the game 21–14.

costumed mascot. Albert was joined by Alberta, a female alligator mascot, in 1986.

Uga: The Most Recognized Football Mascot

Some stories say the "Georgia Bulldogs" name has been around since the late 1800s. However, the name most likely became popular in the 1920s, when newspaper reporters in Atlanta began to use it frequently. Since 1955, there have been five bulldog mascots named Uga (short for the University of Georgia). Uga has had his picture taken with the governor of Georgia. He's even visited the Georgia

Georgia mascot Uga stands guard in the end zone during a 2006 game. Uga may look tough, but he is known to be a very friendly bulldog that loves children.

House of Representatives and received the key to the city of Savannah! In 1997, Uga appeared on the cover of *Sports Illustrated*.

Wildcats in Kentucky

The wildcat became the official mascot of the University of Kentucky football team in 1909. After a big win that year, Commandant Carbusier, head of the university's military department, declared that the team had "fought like wildcats." The name stuck.

Today, there are three official mascots. Blue is a live bobcat (commonly called a wildcat) who lives at the Salato Wildlife Education

Center near Frankfort, Kentucky. Blue does not attend games because bobcats are shy animals and do not like crowds. The Wildcat, introduced in 1976, is a costumed mascot who roams the sidelines during games. Scratch, another costumed Wildcat, concentrates on entertaining children.

Fighting Roosters

Gamecocks, or fighting roosters, are known to be both vicious and persistent fighters. Rooster fights, known as cock fights, were once popular in the United States but have been outlawed due to their cruelty. Around 1900, however, fans began referring to the University of South Carolina football team as the "Game Cocks." The name "Gamecocks" became official in 1903.

The South Carolina mascot is a costumed gamecock named Cocky. In 1980, Cocky took over for the previous costumed mascot, Big Spur. Cocky was chosen National Mascot of the Year in 1986, 1994, and 2004.

Smokey Leads the Volunteers

In 1953, the student body at the University of Tennessee voted on a live mascot for their football team. They chose a Bluetick Coonhound, a Tennessee native breed. At halftime during a game, several coonhounds were led onto the field, and the crowd cheered for the one it wanted to be the new mascot. When the crowd cheered for the last dog, the dog barked back! This made the crowd cheer even louder, and the dog howled in response. This is how Smokey was chosen as the Tennessee Volunteers' mascot. Since 1953, there have been eight Smokeys, all Bluetick Coonhounds.

Mr. C

Vanderbilt University was founded by shipping magnate Cornelius Vanderbilt in 1873. Vanderbilt had long before earned the nickname "Commodore" because he used boats to deliver supplies to forts during the War of 1812. This became the nickname and mascot of the football team. Mr. Commodore, or Mr. C, looks like an eighteenth-century naval officer. He wears a naval uniform and carries a sword.

The Crimson Tide

Around 1907, a sports editor of the *Birmingham Age-Herald* referred to the Alabama team as "the Crimson Tide." He used the term to describe the dominating way in which the team played during a game against their rivals, Auburn. When these two teams met again in 1948, they played on a field of red mud. After a 6–6 tie, "Crimson Tide" became the favorite nickname with fans.

Alabama's mascot is an elephant. In 1930, a reporter referred to the Alabama players as "elephants" after they beat another team 64–0. Sometimes the team is called the red elephants. The costumed mascot is named Big Al.

Here Come the Hogs

In 1909, coach Hugo Bezdek called his Arkansas squad a "wild band of razorback hogs" after a 16–0 win over LSU. Today, they are affectionately called "The Hogs" by their fans. The Razorbacks have four costumed mascots. Big Red is the "Fighting Razorback" that represents the Arkansas fighting spirit. Sue E. entertains the crowd with dances and costume changes. Pork Chop is a youthful version of the

Boss Hog—standing at 9 feet tall (2.7 meters)—is ready for the Arkansas Razorbacks to take the field at Donald W. Reynolds Razorback Stadium. Boss Hog joined the team at the end of the 1998–1999 season.

Razorback mascot, and Boss Hog is a nine-foot-tall inflatable mascot. The Razorbacks also have had a live mascot since the 1960s. The current mascot, Tusk I, is a Russian boar that lives on a nearby farm. Tusk joins the team for every home game.

Aubie and Nova

Aubie the tiger originated as a cartoon on an Auburn football program in 1959. Starting in 1979, a costumed Aubie joined the Auburn team on the sidelines. Aubie has won six Universal Cheerleaders Association (UCA) mascot national championships—

more than any other college football mascot. The Tigers also have a live mascot, a golden eagle. War Eagle VII, nicknamed "Nova," is the seventh Auburn War Eagle. Veterinary students in a raptor center on the campus care for Nova. Before every home game, War Eagle VII circles the stadium and lands at center field.

An Intimidating Mascot

In 1936, LSU purchased a Bengal Tiger with the help of student contributions. The tiger was named Mike, after its trainer. There have been five Mike the Tigers since then. Mike is housed in a building near the LSU stadium. Before each home game, Mike's cage is positioned in front of the opposing team's locker room. Then it is wheeled onto the field while cheerleaders sit atop it. Tradition says that LSU will score a touchdown every time Mike growls. In addition to Mike, a costumed tiger mascot is present at every LSU game.

Bully the Bulldog

The bulldog has been linked to the Mississippi State program since the early 1900s. The team got their first English bulldog mascot, Bully, in 1935. Unfortunately, Bully was killed by a bus in 1939. Students mourned the mascot's death during an extravagant funeral, and the dog was buried beneath the players' bench at the fifty-yard-line. Over the years, the team has had nineteen bulldog mascots, each named Bully. Bully attends every home game. The team also has a costumed bulldog that goes by the same name.

Key Games in the SEC

Each SEC team plays twelve regular-season games, eight of which are games within the conference. Five games are against the other members of the division, and three games are against teams from the other division. Each team is paired with a "rival" from the other division. These rivals (which are not necessarily traditional rivals) meet once every year. The other two interdivisional games change from year to year.

In addition to these games, each team plays four games with teams from other conferences. Some of these matchups change every year. Others, however, remain mostly the same in order to preserve long-standing rivalries. Florida and Florida State, for example, began playing each other in 1902, and have played yearly since 1959. Georgia and Georgia Tech also have a long-standing battle. They have played each other nearly every year for more than 100 years.

The SEC Championship Game

In 1992, the SEC was the first NCAA conference to establish a championship game. It takes place every year and pits the best team from the Eastern Division against the best team from the Western Division. Florida has the most SEC Championship wins, with six. Alabama, Georgia, LSU, and Tennessee all have won two championships, and Auburn has won one.

The first five SEC Championships were dominated by Florida and Alabama. This changed in 1997 when neither team made it to the championship game. Tennessee, led by the wide receiver Peerless Price, won two championships in row. In 1997, they beat Auburn in a close game, 30–29. In 1998, they triumphed over Mississippi State, 24–14, and went on to win the National Championship.

Florida made their sixth trip to the SEC Championship in 2006. They met Arkansas in a wild and exciting match. Florida freshman Percy Harvin was named MVP of the game. He caught a thirty-seven-yard pass, then ran sixty-seven yards to score a touchdown. Although Arkansas came back from a 17–0 deficit, it wasn't enough to beat the mighty Florida Gators, who won 38–28. The Gators went on to win the National Championship against Ohio State, 41–14.

SEC Rivalries

Just as in all college football conferences, the SEC has a long-standing tradition of rivalries with other conference teams. Some of these rivalries began more than 100 years ago. The matchups that follow are some of the more heated rivalries of the SEC.

Auburn won its fifth straight Iron Bowl, beating Alabama 22–15, on November 18, 2006. The team hadn't won five consecutive Iron Bowls since 1958. Above, Auburn's defensive back Jonathan Wilhite tackles Alabama's Keith Brown.

Auburn and Alabama

The Auburn-Alabama rivalry is the most well-known rivalry in the SEC and one of the most heated rivalries in college football. It is also an intense intra-state rivalry. Their typically dramatic matchup is usually scheduled as the last game of the season. The "Iron Bowl," as it is known, is a hot topic in Alabama year round.

Auburn and Alabama first played each other in 1893. Arguments about referees and expenses developed between the teams in the early 1900s, and they stopped playing each other after the 1907 season. For years, football fans in Alabama urged the two schools to reconcile, but the teams refused. In 1948, state politicians threatened to withhold funding for both schools unless they agreed to meet in a yearly game. That year Auburn and Alabama met for the first time in four decades at a neutral site—Birmingham, Alabama. Alabama crushed Auburn 55–0, and the rivalry was back with a vengeance! Today, Alabama leads the series 38–32–1. The Iron Bowl remains one of the biggest annual events in the state of Alabama.

Tennessee and Alabama

Tennessee considers Alabama to be its greatest rival. Alabama is the only SEC team to have won more games, SEC Championships, and National Championships than Tennessee. The rivalry dates back to the 1920s, when Tennessee first started to challenge Alabama's dominance. The yearly matchup became known as the "Third Saturday in October," although it is not always held on that day. Although Alabama leads the series 44–38–7, Tennessee has recorded several historic wins against the tough Crimson Tide. For example, in 1995, Tennessee quarterback Peyton Manning led the Vols to a decisive 41–14 victory, ending a nine-year Alabama winning streak.

Mississippi and Ole Miss

Prior to 1926, Mississippi State dominated Ole Miss on the football field, outscoring them 327–33 in thirteen consecutive games. However, after Ole Miss beat Mississippi State in 1926, hostilities between the two schools grew. In order to keep future games peaceful, the Ole Miss Honor Society proposed that a trophy be awarded to the winner of the matchup every year, and that both school anthems be sung. The trophy, the "Golden Egg," is a gold-plated football on a pedestal. Ole Miss won the first Golden Egg. In 1977, the yearly

Ole Miss/Mississippi State game was dubbed the "Egg Bowl."

Arkansas and LSU

Arkansas and LSU played each other every year from 1906 to 1936, and then from 1953 to 1956. Since Arkansas joined the SEC in 1992, the two teams have battled it out to be the best in the West Division of the conference. Starting in 1996, the winner of the annual matchup has been awarded the "Golden Boot." (This trophy is shaped like Arkansas and Louisiana together, which resembles a boot.) It is made of gold and weighs close to a

On October 29, 2005, Georgia quarterback Joe Tereshinski makes a spectacular touchdown catch over the head of the Florida defender Jervis Herring.

whopping 200 pounds. So far, LSU leads the Battle for the Golden Boot, eight games to three.

Georgia and . . . Everyone

Of all the SEC rivalries, those between Georgia and other teams are perhaps the most memorable. Georgia and Auburn first met on the football field in 1892; Auburn won 10–0. This was the beginning of what is today called the "Deep South's Oldest Rivalry." The two teams have played each other nearly every year since 1898. They met for the 100th time in 1996. The game went into a fourth overtime period before Georgia finally won, 56–49.

Georgia also has a longtime rivalry with the Georgia Tech Yellow Jackets, who used to be members of the SEC. The teams have met 101 times since 1893. Georgia Tech won that first game 28–6. Angry Georgia fans chased the winning team out of town by throwing rocks at them! This was the beginning of the rivalry that has come to be known as "Clean, Old-Fashioned Hate."

Famous Bowl Appearances

1953 Orange Bowl: Alabama 61, Syracuse 6—This game was the first televised Orange Bowl and Syracuse's first-ever appearance in a bowl game. Alabama's margin of victory remains the largest ever in an Orange Bowl. Their gain of 596 total yards was an Orange Bowl record for forty-nine years (until 2002, when Florida gained 659 yards against Maryland). Altogether, the Crimson Tide set seven Orange Bowl records and tied four more.

1984 Hall of Fame Bowl: Kentucky 20, Wisconsin 19—After a difficult first half for the Kentucky Wildcats, the Wisconsin Badgers were ahead 16–7. The Wildcats rallied in the third quarter, however. In eleven plays, they moved eighty-two yards down the field during one drive. Halfway through the third quarter, Kentucky kicker Joey Worley made a fifty-two-yard field goal to put the Wildcats in the lead for the first time. Wisconsin missed a field goal in the final minutes of the game, and the Wildcats hung on for an exciting win.

1991 Sugar Bowl: Tennessee 23, Virginia 22—This was one of the greatest Sugar Bowl comebacks in history. At the end of the first half, Tennessee was losing 16–0. The Vols continued to struggle during the third quarter. In the fourth quarter, Tennessee intercepted the ball and scored a touchdown after eleven plays. This sparked the team, although they were still down 22–17, with just 2:31 minutes left. Led by quarterback Andy Kelly and running back Tony Thomson, the Vols marched down the field, keeping a close eye on the clock. With just thirty seconds remaining, Thomson ran the ball into the end zone, giving them the lead—and the win!

Georgia's rivalry with the Florida Gators began in 1912 when the two teams met in Jacksonville, Florida. With the exception of three games, the matchup has been held there every year. Half of the stadium is filled with cheering Florida fans, and the other half is filled with roaring Georgia fans.

Florida Gators Steven Harris *(left)* and Brandon Siler hold up a National Championship banner after defeating Ohio State in the BCS National Championship Game at the end of the 2006 season.

Still the Dominant Conference

At the end of the 2006 season, nine SEC teams played in bowl games. Six SEC teams won those games, a conference record. Perhaps the most impressive win was the underdog Florida Gators crushing of the Ohio Buckeyes, 41–14, in the BCS National Championship Game. Coincidentally, LSU beat Notre Dame by the same score in the Sugar Bowl. After the bowl games were over, the SEC had the best team (Florida) and the third-best team (LSU) in all of college football. Three SEC teams made it into the top ten, and five more were among the top twenty-five teams. With results like these, it is easy to think that the SEC is the best conference in college football.

GLOSSARY

academic Referring to educational studies or an educational institution.

All-American Selected as one of the best athletes in a college sport.

alma mater The university or college a person attended.

Bowl Championship Series A postseason series of bowl games designed to determine which teams are the best in the nation.

brigadier general The lowest rank of general in the U.S. Army.

center In football, a player on the offensive line who starts each play by handing the ball to the quarterback.

coincide To go with or match something similar.

confederate Having to do with the Confederate States of America—a group of eleven Southern states during the American Civil War.

dominance Complete control over other people or teams.

down One of four consecutive plays in football during which a team must score or advance the ball at least ten yards.

end zone One of two areas at opposite ends of a football field where a ball must be carried or caught to earn points.

fullback A large running back who runs with the ball and blocks for other running backs.

gridiron Another name for a football field.

halfback A running back who is responsible for most of the running plays as well as some passing plays.

lackluster Lacking energy, excitement, or passion.

linebacker A defensive player who lines up five to six feet away from the defensive line before a play begins.

lineman A defensive player who lines up directly on the defensive line before a play begins.

magnate Someone who has a lot of power and wealth, especially someone in a business or industry.

offensive end A player who lines up on the end of the offensive line; commonly called a tight end.

prestigious Having a positive or well-known reputation.

quarterback The leader of the offense who calls plays, starts plays, throws passes, and sometimes runs with the ball.

racism Hatred or prejudice against people who belong to races other than one's own.

raptor A bird of prey, such as a golden eagle.

reconcile To bring about a friendly relationship between people or groups who were fighting.

recruit To take on people as players for your team.

regulate To organize and control something with rules or laws.

revenue Money that comes into a business from the sale of goods or services.

rivalry Continuing competitiveness between people or teams.

rugby A sport in which teammates try to score by passing or handing a ball to one another as the other team tries to stop them from reaching an end zone.

running back An offensive player who lines up behind or next to the quarterback and who runs with the ball.

sack To tackle the quarterback before he can throw the ball, hand it off, or run down the field with it.

tuition The financial cost of attending a school or university.

underdog The team in a matchup that is not expected to win.

vengeance With great force, or to an excessive degree.

wide receiver The pass-catching specialist on the offense.

FOR MORE INFORMATION

National Collegiate Athletic Association (NCAA)
700 W. Washington Street
P.O. Box 6222
Indianapolis, IN 46206-6222
(317) 917-6222
Web site: http://www.ncaa.org

National Football Foundation's College Football Hall of Fame
111 South St. Joseph Street
South Bend, IN 46601
(800) 440-FAME (3263)
Web site: http://www.collegefootball.org

Southeastern Conference (SEC)
2201 Richard Arrington Boulevard North
Birmingham, AL 35203
(205) 458-3000
Web site: http://www.secsports.com

Web Sites

Due to the changing nature of Internet links, Rosen Publishing has developed an online list of Web sites related to the subject of this book. This site is updated regularly. Please use this link to access the list:

http://www.rosenlinks.com/icfo/fsec

FOR FURTHER READING

Bradley, Michael. *Big Games: College Football's Greatest Rivalries*. Dulles, VA: Potomac Books, 2006.

DeCock, Luke. *Great Teams in College Football History*. Chicago, IL: Raintree Publishing, 2006.

Ours, Robert M. *Bowl Games: College Football's Greatest Tradition*. Yardley, PA: Westholme Publishing, 2004.

Pellowski, Michael J. *The Little Giant Book of Football Facts*. New York, NY: Sterling Publishing, 2005.

Savage, Jeff. *Top 10 Heisman Trophy Winners*. Berkeley Heights, NJ: Enslow Publishers, 1999.

Warner, Chris. *SEC Sports History & Tradition Collection*. Baton Rouge, LA: CEW Enterprises, 2001.

Warner, Chris. *SEC Sports Quotes*. Baton Rouge, LA: CEW Enterprises, 2002.

BIBLIOGRAPHY

Auburn University. "Wreck Tech Pajama Parade, Pep Rally Set for Friday Evening." August 5, 2005. Retrieved December 12, 2006 (http://www.ocm.auburn.edu/news_releases/wrecktech05.html).

Hannon, Kent. "Herschel's in the Hall." University of Georgia. Retrieved January 7, 2007 (http://www.uga.edu/gm/300/FeatHerschel.html).

Malumphy, Chris. "Drafts by College." DraftHistory.com. Retrieved January 11, 2007 (http://www.drafthistory.com/colleges.html).

Mississippi State Bulldogs. "Sylvester Croom—Head Football Coach." Retrieved December 14, 2006 (http://www.mstateathletics.com/index.php?s=&change_well_id=2&url_article_id=4521).

NCAA.org. "History." Retrieved December 11, 2006 (http://www.ncaa.org/about/history.html).

Orangebowl.com. "Offensive Showcase for Gators." Retrieved January 24, 2007 (http://www.orangebowl.org/OB.php?sec=years&year=2002).

O'Sullivan, Dan. "1991 Tennessee 23, Virginia 22." BCSfootball.com. December 13, 2002. Retrieved January 24, 2007 (http://espn.go.com/abcsports/bcs/sugar/s/1991.html).

Profootballhof.com. "Hall of Famers by College." Retrieved January 9, 2007 (http://www.profootballhof.com/hof/colleges.html).

SECsports.com. "Florida Wins 2006 SEC Championship Game, 38–28." December 2, 2006. "Saban Embraces Alabama's High Expectations." January 4, 2007. "SEC Football Record Book—Individuals." "SEC National Championship, Bowl and Poll Notes." January 9, 2007. "Sweet Victory: LSU Downs Irish in Sugar Bowl, 41–14." January 4, 2007. Retrieved January 2007 (http://www.secsports.com).

Ukathletic.com. "1984 Hall of Fame Bowl." December 29, 1984. Retrieved January 24, 2007 (http://www.ukathletics.com/index.php?s=&change_well_id=2&url_article_id=7201#1984).

University of South Carolina. "Steve Spurrier: Profile." Retrieved January 19, 2007 (http://uscsports.cstv.com/sports/m-footbl/mtt/spurrier_steve00.html).

Universty of Tennessee. "Robert R. Neyland History Page." Retrieved December 13, 2006 (http://web.utk.edu/~finaid/newpage/neyland-hist.html).

Walsh, Christopher J. *Where Football Is King: A History of the SEC*. Lanham, MD: Taylor Trade Publishing, 2006.

Warner, Chris. *A Tailgater's Guide to SEC Football*. Baton Rouge, LA: CEW Enterprises, 2004.

INDEX

About the Author

Greg Roza is a writer and editor who specializes in creating library books and other educational materials. He lives in Hamburg, New York, with his wife, Abigail, son, Lincoln, and daughters Autumn and Daisy. Roza has a master's degree in English from SUNY Fredonia, and loves to stay in shape by participating in athletic activities.

Photo Credits

Cover top, bottom, pp. 19, 22, 30, 33, 39, 41 © Getty Images; pp. 1, 3, 6, 14, 21, 28, 35 Shutterstock; pp. 4–5, 15 University of Tennessee; pp. 7, 17, 25, 27, 40 © www.istockphotos.com/Todd Bates; pp. 9, 10, 16 Paul W. Bryant Museum/The University of Alabama; p. 18 University of Florida; p. 24 © Focus on Sport/Getty Images; p. 26 © Collegiate Images/Getty Images; p. 29 Ron Irby; p. 37 © AP Images.

Designer: Tom Forget
Photo Researcher: Marty Levick